Simple 1-2-3™
HALLOWEEN
COLOR & FRAME

Simple 1-2-3 is a trademark of Publications International, Ltd.
New Seasons is a registered trademark of Publications International, Ltd.

Copyright © 2021 Publications International, Ltd. All rights reserved.
This book may not be reproduced or quoted in whole or in part by any
means whatsoever without written permission from:

Louis Weber, CEO
Publications International, Ltd.
8140 Lehigh Ave
Morton Grove, IL 60053

Images from Shutterstock.com

Permission is never granted for commercial purposes.

ISBN: 978-1-64558-717-0

Manufactured in China.

8 7 6 5 4 3 2 1

Let's get social!

@Publications_International
@PublicationsInternational
www.pilbooks.com

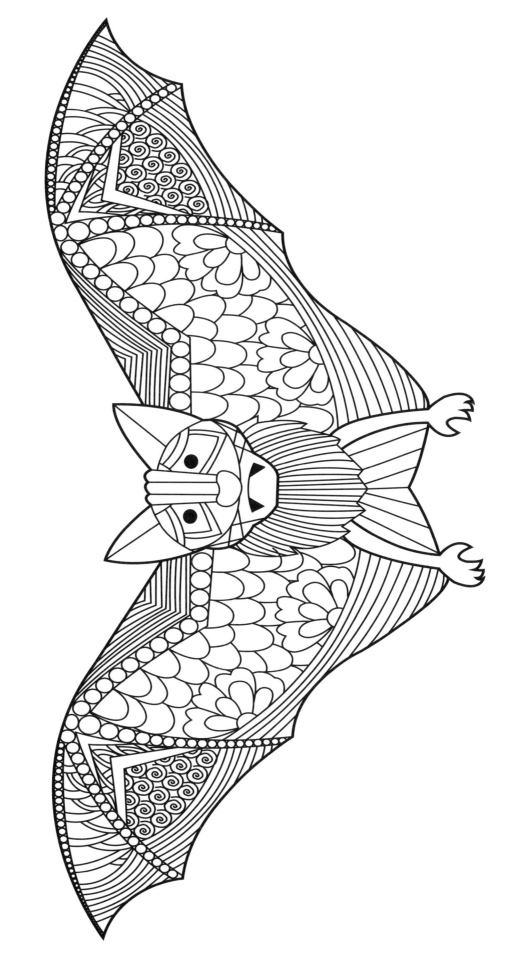

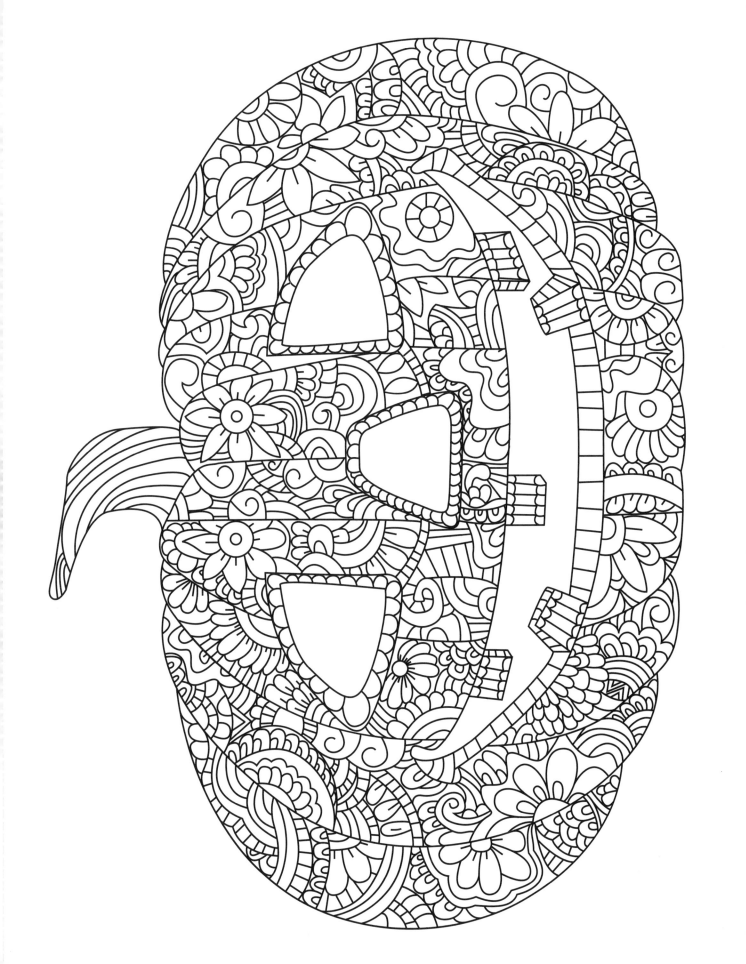

HAPPY HALLOWEEN

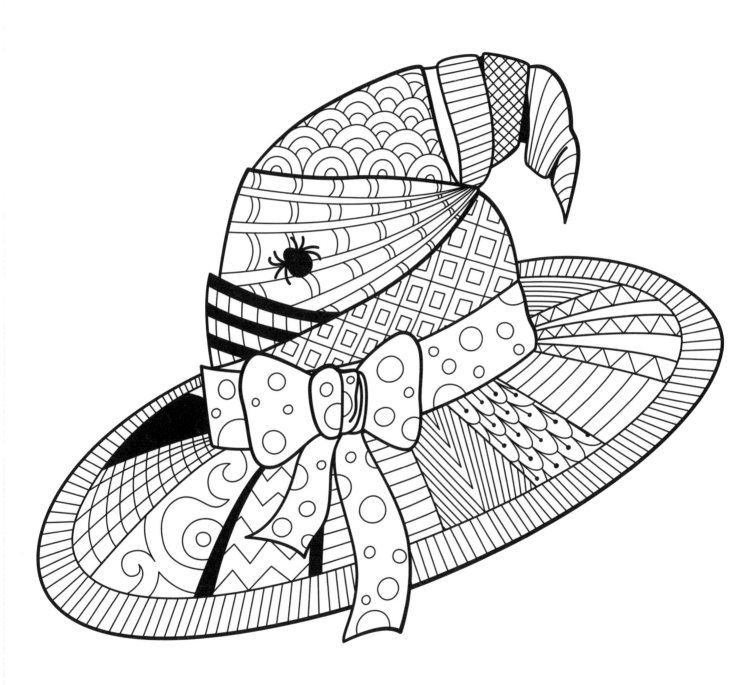